Although the author and publisher have made every effort to ensure that the information in this book was correct at press time, the author and publisher do not assume and hereby disclaim any liability to any party for any loss, damage, or disruption caused by errors or omissions, whether such errors or omissions result from negligence, accident, or any other cause.

This book is presented solely for educational and entertainment purposes. The author and publisher are not offering it as a form of opinion of any sort.

On WINNING

"We will have so much winning if I get elected that you may get bored with winning."

"When someone crosses you, my advice is Get Even! That is not typical advice, but it is real life advice. If you do not get even, you are just a schmuck! When people wrong you, go after those people because it is a good feeling and because other people will see you doing it. I love getting even. I get screwed all the time. I go after people, and you know what? People do not play around with me as much as they do with others."

We are going to start winning big on trade. Militarily, we're going to build up our military. We're going to have such a strong military that nobody, nobody is going to mess with us. We're not going to have to use it."

In GENERAL

"The Bible is the most special thing."

"Well, I'll tell you what. The Koran is very interesting. A lot of people say it teaches love and there is a very big group of people who really understand the Koran far better than I do. I'm certainly not an expert, to put it mildly. But there's something there that teaches some very negative vibe. I mean things are happening, when you look at people blowing up all over the streets that are in some of the countries over in the Middle East, just blowing up a super market with not even soldiers, just people, when 250 people die in a super market that are shopping, where people die in a store or in a street. There's a lot of hatred there that's some place. Now I don't know if that's from the Koran. I don't know if that's from some place else. But there's tremendous hatred out there that I've never seen anything like it. So, you have two views. You have the view that the Koran is all about love and then you have the view that the Koran is, that there's a lot of hate in the Koran."

"And our real unemployment is anywhere from 18 to 20 percent. Don't believe the 5.6. Don't believe it."

"The world is a horrible place. Lions kill for food, but **people kill for sport**. People try to kill you mentally, especially if you are on top. We all have friends that want everything we have. They want our money, our business, house, car, wife and dog. Those are our friends. Our enemies are even worse! You have to protect yourself in life."

"Islamic terrorism is heating up!"

"They built a hotel. When I build a hotel, I have to pay interest. They don't have to pay interest because they took the oil when we left Iraq, I said we should have taken. So now ISIS has the oil."

"Last week I read 2,300 Humvees — these are big vehicles, they were left behind for the enemy. You would say maybe two, maybe four? Twenty-three hundred sophisticated vehicles."

"I could stand in the middle of 5th Avenue, and shoot somebody and I wouldn't lose voters."

"We won with poorly educated. I love the poorly educated."

"Healthy young child goes to doctor, gets pumped with massive shot of many vaccines, doesn't feel good and changes — autism. Many such cases!" *(disregarding scientific research to the contrary)*

"We build a school, we build a road, they blow up the school, we build another school, we build another road they blow them up, we build again, in the meantime we can't get a fucking school in Brooklyn."

"I saw a report yesterday. There's so much oil, all over the world, they don't know where to dump it. And Saudi Arabia says, 'Oh, there's too much oil.' Do you think they're our friends? They're not our friends."

"Sadly the American dream is dead. But if I get elected president, I will bring it back bigger and better and stronger than ever before and we will make America great again."

"I will be the greatest jobs president that God ever created. I will bring back our jobs from China, from Mexico, from Japan, from so many places. I'll bring back our jobs and I'll bring back our money."

"I watch the speeches of these people, and they say the sun will rise, the moon will set, all sorts of wonderful things will happen, and people are saying, 'What is going on? I just want a job.'"

"Doctors are quitting. I have a friend who is a doctor, and he said to me the other day, 'Donald, I never saw anything like it. I have more accountants than I have nurses.'"

"Well, somebody's doing the raping, Don. I mean somebody's doing it. Who's doing the raping? Who's doing the raping?"

"There's nobody bigger or better at the military than I am."

"Watch and study the mosques, because a lot of talk is going on at the mosques."

On the REPUBLICAN CAMPAIGN

"We have something special going on in the Republican party. And, unfortunately, the people in the party, they call them the elites or they call them whatever they call them. But those are the people that don't respect it yet. We have millions and millions of people, I've discussed it before. We have millions and millions of people coming up and voting, largely for me.
It's a record. It has never happened before. In 100 years what is happening now to the Republican party has never happened before."

"The other candidates — they went in, they didn't know the air conditioning didn't work. They sweated like dogs...How are they gonna beat ISIS? I don't think it's gonna happen."

"Everybody's got to be covered. This is an un-Republican thing for me to say . . . I am going to take care of everybody. I don't care if it costs me votes or not. Everybody's going to be taken care of much better than they're taken care of now."

"Well, you need somebody, because politicians are all talk and no action. They will not bring us — believe me — to the Promised Land."

On IMMIGRATION and MIGRATION and REFUGEES

"Donald J. Trump is calling for a total and complete shutdown of Muslims entering the United States."

"I hate the concept of it, but on a humanitarian basis, you have to. It's living in hell in Syria. There's no question about it. They're living in hell, and something has to be done."

"What can be simpler or more accurately stated?
The Mexican government is forcing their most unwanted people into the United States. They are, in many cases, criminals, drug dealers, rapists, etcetera. ..."

"When Mexico sends its people, they're not sending the best. They're not sending you, they're sending people that have lots of problems and they're bringing those problems with us. They're bringing drugs. They're bringing crime. They're rapists... And some, I assume, are good people."

"I will build a great wall — and nobody builds walls better than me, believe me —and I'll build them very inexpensively. I will build a great, great wall on our southern border, and I will make Mexico pay for that wall. Mark my words."

"A nation without borders is not a nation at all. We must have a wall. The rule of law matters."

"Mexico will pay for it, because they are not doing us any favors. They could stop all of this illegal trade if they wanted to immediately. Mexico will pay for the wall. It's a small portion of the kind of money that we lose and the deficits that we have with Mexico."

When revealing he will charge the Mexican government an estimated 10 - 12 billion dollars to build a wall to divide the country's borders and their complete refusal to do so.

"I will, and the wall just got 10 feet taller, believe me."

"Oh, well, if you look at the statistics, of people coming— I didn't say about Mexico— I say the *illegal immigrants*— if you look at the statistics on rape, on crime, on everything, coming in illegally into this country, they're mind-boggling. If you go to Fusion, you will see a story about 80% of the women coming in– I mean, you have to take a look at these stories. And you know who owns Fusion? Univision. It was in *The Huffington Post*. I said, let me get some of these articles because I've heard some horrible things. I deal a lot of talking with people on the border patrol. They're incredible people. They help our country."

"This guy used a filthy, disgusting word on television, and he should be ashamed of himself, and he should apologize, OK? Number one. Number two, we have a trade deficit with Mexico of $58 billion a year. And that doesn't include all the drugs that are pouring across and destroying our country. We're going to make them pay for that wall. Now, the wall is $10 billion to $12 billion, if I do it. If these guys do it, it'll end up costing $200 billion."

"Our leaders are stupid. Our politicians are stupid. And the Mexican government is much smarter, much sharper, much more cunning, and they send the bad ones over because they don't wanna pay for them, they don't wanna take care of them, why should they when the stupid leaders of the United States are doing it for them?"

"They're going to build a plant and illegals are going drive those cars right over the border. And they'll probably end up stealing the cars."

"I'm putting the people on notice that are coming here from Syria as part of this mass migration, that if I win, if I win, they're going back."

DONALD on DONALD

"Back in 1991 the markets were terrible, and everyone was going out of business. I was in deep, deep trouble. I owed billions of dollars. Sure, I could tell you all I want about how to handle pressure well, but I owed many banks billions of dollars. It was not exactly fun. Believe me, it is not cool to be Donald Trump when you owe billions of dollars."

"People are so shocked when they find ... out I am Protestant. I am Presbyterian. And I go to church and I love God and I love my church."

"It's very hard for them to attack me on looks, because I'm so good looking."

"The final key to the way I promote is bravado. I play to people's fantasies. People may not always think big themselves, but they can still get very excited by those who do. That's why a little hyperbole never hurts."

"One of the key problems today is that politics is such a disgrace. Good people don't go into government."

"My fingers are long and beautiful, as, it has been well documented, are various other parts of my body."

"Look at those hands, are they small hands? And, *(Republican rival Marco Rubio)* referred to my hands: 'If they're small, something else must be small.' I guarantee you there's no problem. I guarantee."

"The point is, you can never be too greedy."

"My Twitter has become so powerful that I can actually make my enemies tell the truth."

"I'm owned by the people! I mean, I'm telling you, I'm no angel, but I'm gonna do right by them!"

"My IQ is one of the highest — and you all know it! Please don't feel so stupid or insecure; it's not your fault."

"So I've been doing deals for a long time. I've been making lots of wonderful deals, great deals. That's what I do. Never, ever, ever in my life have I seen any transaction so incompetently negotiated as our deal with Iran. And I mean never."

"I have so many websites, I have them all over the place, I hire people, they do a website, it costs me $3."

"I don't need anybody's money ... I'm using my own money, I'm not using the lobbyists, I'm not using donors, I don't care. I'm really rich."

"Sorry losers and haters, but my IQ is one of the highest — and you all know it!"

"I have a great relationship with the Blacks. I've always had a great relationship with the Blacks."

"The beauty of me is that I'm very rich."

"I will be the greatest jobs president that God ever created. I will bring back our jobs from China, from Mexico, from Japan, from so many places. I'll bring back our jobs and I'll bring back our money."

"I'm proud of my net worth, I've done an amazing job ... The total is $8,737,540,000 US. I'm not doing that to brag, because you know what, I don't have to brag."

"I think I am a nice person. People that know me like me. Does my family like me? I think so ... I think I'm actually a very nice person."

"I have said things that I could've held back. But not that often, surprisingly not that often, but certainly there have been occasions."

"As everybody knows, but the haters and losers refuse to acknowledge, I do not wear a "wig." My hair may not be perfect, but it's mine."

"I don't have a racist bone in my body."

"Love him or hate him, Donald Trump is a man who is certain about what he wants and sets out to get it, no holds barred. Women find his power almost as much of a turn-on as his money." *(Donald Trump)*

"I don't think I've made mistakes. Every time somebody said I made a mistake, they do the polls and my numbers go up, so I guess I haven't made any mistakes."

"These are stupid people that say, 'Oh didn't Trump declare bankruptcy? Didn't he go bankrupt?' I didn't go bankrupt."

"All I know is I have a very big group of support, and I think one of the reasons is the people don't trust you, and the people don't trust the media. And I understand why."

"15,000 people showed up to hear me speak. Bigger than anybody and everybody knows it. A beautiful day with incredible people that were wonderful, great Americans, I will tell you. John McCain goes, "Oh, boy, Trump makes my job difficult. He had 15,000 *crazies* show up." Crazies. He called them all crazy. I said, they weren't crazy. They were great Americans. These people. If you would have seen these people— you— I know what a crazy is. I know all about crazies. These weren't crazy. So he insulted me and he insulted everybody in that room..."

"I'm not a schmuck. Even if the world goes to hell in a hand basket, I won't lose a penny."

"We're stupid people, we're being led by stupid people, and we're stupid because we allow these people to get into office."

"Love him or hate him, Trump is a man who is certain about what he wants and sets out to get it, no holds barred. Women find his power almost as much of a turn-on as his money."

"I wish I'd had a great marriage. See, my father was always very proud of me, but the one thing he got right was that he had a great marriage. He was married for 64 years. One of my ex-wives once said to me, 'You have to work at a marriage.' And I said, 'That's the most ridiculous thing.'"

"The old rich may look down their noses at me, but I think they kiss my ass."

On SUCCESS

"Success appears to happen overnight because we all see stories in newspapers and on TV about previously unknown people who have suddenly become famous. But consider a sequoia tree that has been growing for several hundred years. Just because a television crew one day decides to do a story about that tree doesn't mean it didn't exist before."

"One of the **problems when you become successful is that jealousy and envy inevitably follow.** There are people -- I categorize them as life's losers -- who get their sense of accomplishment and achievement from trying to stop others. As far as I'm concerned, if they had any real ability, they wouldn't be fighting me, they'd be doing something constructive themselves."

"If you can't get rich dealing with politicians, there's something wrong with you."

We are going to turn this country around. We are going to win bigly on trade, militarily... we're going to build up our military. We're going to have such a strong military that nobody, nobody is going to mess with us... we're not going to have to use it.

"Part of being a winner is knowing when enough is enough. Sometimes you have to give up the fight and walk away, and move on to something that's more productive."

"Get going. Move forward. Aim High. Plan a takeoff. Don't just sit on the runway and hope someone will come along and push the airplane. It simply won't happen. Change your attitude and gain some altitude. Believe me, you'll love it up here."

On POLITICAL CORRECTNESS

"I think the big problem this country has is being politically correct. I've been challenged by so many people, and I don't frankly have time for total political correctness. And to be honest with you, this country doesn't have time either."

"I am what I am. I am what I am."

"We're going to protect Christianity, and I can say that. I don't have to be politically correct. We're going to protect it."

"If I'm president, you're going to see 'Merry Christmas' in department stores, believe me."

"But we're fighting a very politically correct war. And the other thing is with the terrorists. You have to take out their families. When you get these terrorists, you have to take out their families. They care about their lives. Don't kid yourself. But they say they don't care about their lives. You have to take out their families."

On FOREIGN POLICY and other BUSINESS/COUNTRIES AND RELIGION

"When you have people that are cutting Christians' heads off, when you have a world, at the border and in so many places … that it's medieval times … We don't have time for tone. We have to go out and get the job done."

"China's Communist Party has now publicly praised Obama's reelection. They have never had it so good. Will own America soon."

"Free trade is terrible. Free trade can be wonderful if you have smart people. But we have stupid people."

"Listen you motherfucker, we're going to tax you 25 percent!" (China exports)

"And by the way, many, many, most Muslims are wonderful people, but is there a Muslim problem? Look what's happening. Look what happened right here in my city with the World Trade Center and lots of other places. So I said it and I thought it was going to be very controversial but actually it was very well received. I think people want the truth. I think they're tired of politicians. They're tired of politically correct stuff."

"I keep asking, how long will we go on defending South Korea from North Korea without payment? South Korea is a very very rich country. They're rich because of us. They sell us televisions, they sell us cars. They sell us everything. They are making a fortune. We have a huge deficit with South Korea. They're friends of mine. I do deals with them. I've been partners with them, no problem. But they think we're stupid. They can't believe it. We are defending them against North Korea, we're doing it for nothing. We're not in that position. When will they start to pay us for this defense? Isn't it really ridiculous when you think of it? They make a fortune on the United States and then they got some problems, and what happens? They call the United States to defend them, and we get nothing?"

"This could be one of the great military coups of all time if they send them to our country -- young, strong people and they turn out to be ISIS. Now, probably that won't happen, but some of them definitely in my opinion will be ISIS."

"I mean, look at Libya. Look at Iraq. Iraq used to be no terrorists. He (Hussein) would kill the terrorists immediately, which is like now it's the Harvard of terrorism. If you look at Iraq from years ago, I'm not saying he was a nice guy, he was a horrible guy, but it was a lot better than it is right now. Right now, Iraq is a training ground for terrorists. Right now Libya, nobody even knows Libya, frankly there is no Iraq and there is no Libya. It's all broken up. They have no control. Nobody knows what's going on."

"Well, that is a 'gotcha' question, though. I mean, you know when you're asking me about who's running this, this, this... I will be so good at the military, your head will spin." *(on the different factions of militant groups in the Middle East)*

"We're going to knock the shit out of ISIS."

"They [ISIS] just built a hotel in Syria. Can you believe this? They built a hotel. When I have to build a hotel, I pay interest. They don't have to pay interest, because they took the oil that, when we left Iraq, I said we should've taken."

"Mexico's totally corrupt gov't looks horrible with El Chapo's escape—totally corrupt. U.S. paid them $3 billion."

"You look at the Middle East, they're chopping off heads, they're chopping off the heads of Christians and anybody else that happens to be in the way, they're drowning people in steel cages, and now we're talking about water boarding. ... It's fine, and if we want to go stronger, I'd go stronger too."

"The United States is bound by laws and treaties and I will not order our military or other officials to violate those laws and will seek their advice on such matters. I will not order a military officer to disobey the law. It is clear that as president I will be bound by laws just like all Americans and I will meet those responsibilities."

"We're going to stay within the laws. But you know what we're going to do? We're going to have those laws broadened."

On PROMISES – PROMISES

"Ladies and gentlemen, I am officially running for President of the United States, and we are going to make our country great again."

"I'll win the Latino vote because I'll create jobs. I'll create jobs and the Latinos will have jobs they didn't have."

"I would bomb the hell out of those oilfields. I wouldn't send many troops because you won't need 'em by the time I'm finished."

"We need somebody who can take the brand of the United States and make it great again. Ladies and gentlemen: I am officially running for president of the United States, and we are going to make our country great again."

"New Hampshire has a tremendous drug epidemic. I am going to create borders. No drugs are coming in. We're going to build a wall . . . They will stop coming to New Hampshire. They will stop coming to our country."

"We're gonna bring businesses back. We're gonna have businesses that used to be in New Hampshire, that are now in Mexico, come back to New Hampshire, and you can tell them to go fuck themselves. Because they let you down, and they left!"

"I will build you ... one of the great ballrooms of the world."

"We're going to be looking at a lot of different things. A lot of people are saying that and a lot of people are saying that bad things are happening out there. We're going to be looking at that and a lot of different things."

On BEING ATTACKED AS A NATION

"I really am convinced we're in danger of the sort of terrorist attacks that will make the bombing of the Trade Center look like kids playing with firecrackers."

"We lose everywhere. We lose militarily. We can't beat ISIS – give me a break."

"I'm the worst thing that's ever happened to ISIS."

"I would certainly implement that. Absolutely."
(implementation of a Muslim tracking data base in United States)

"I watched when the World Trade Center came tumbling down. And I watched in Jersey City, New Jersey, where thousands and thousands of people were cheering as that building was coming down. Thousands of people were cheering."

"When you get these terrorists, you have to take out their families . . . When they say they don't care about their lives, you have to take out their families."

"They have sections in Paris that are radicalized, where the police refuse to go there. They're petrified. The police refuse to go in there."

"I would bring back waterboarding, and I would bring back a hell of a lot worse than waterboarding. You can rest assured that as commander in chief, I would use whatever enhanced interrogation methods we could to keep this country safe."

"Torture works, okay folks? Believe me, it works.(...)Waterboarding is your minor form. Some people say it's not actually torture. Let's assume it is. But they asked me the question. What do you think of waterboarding? Absolutely fine. But we should go much stronger than waterboarding. That's the way I feel."

"Without looking at the various polling data, it is obvious to anybody the hatred is beyond comprehension. Where this hatred comes from and why we will have to determine. Until we are able to determine and understand this problem and the dangerous threat it poses, our country cannot be the victims of horrendous attacks by people that believe only in Jihad, and have no sense of reason or respect for human life."

"The other thing with the terrorists is you have to take out their families, when you get these terrorists, you have to take out their families. They care about their lives, don't kid

yourself. When they say they don't care about their lives, you have to take out their families."

"I would just bomb those suckers, and that's right, I'd blow up the pipes, I'd blow up the refineries, I'd blow up every single inch, there would be nothing left." *(fighting the Islamic State)*

On GUNS

"By the way, it was a gun-free zone. Let me tell you, if you had a couple teachers with guns in that room, you would have been a hell of a lot better off."

"Get rid of gun free zones. The four great marines who were just shot never had a chance. They were highly trained but helpless without guns."

"I generally oppose gun control, but I support the ban on assault weapons and I also support a slightly longer waiting period to purchase a gun. With today's internet technology we should be able to tell within 72 hours if a potential gun owner has a record."

"I would also add that hunters contribute more to the preservation of game animals and their habitat than any of these protesters. Hunters are the original conservationists. To see this historically you have to look no further then Teddy Roosevelt and his creation of the National Parks System."

"There's an assault on the Second Amendment. You know Obama's going to do an executive order and really knock the hell out of it," Trump said. "You know, the system's supposed to be you get the Democrats, you get the Republicans, and you make deals. He can't do that. He can't do that. So he's going to sign another executive order having to do with the Second Amendment, having to do with guns. I will veto. I will unsign that so fast."

"I do not support expanding background checks. The current background checks do not work."

On THE PRESIDENT – *Barack Obama*

"I wonder if President Obama would have attended the funeral of Justice Scalia if it were held in a Mosque? Very sad that he did not go."

"The U.S. will invite El Chapo, the Mexican drug lord who just escaped prison, to become a U.S. citizen because our "leaders" can't say no!" *(Tweet)(joke?)*

"He has done nothing for African-Americans. You look at what's gone on with their income levels. You look at what's gone on with their youth. I thought that he would be a great cheerleader for this country. I thought he'd do a fabulous job for the African-American citizens of this country. He has done nothing."

"Your brother's administration gave us Barack Obama because it was such a disaster those last 3 months that Abraham Lincoln couldn't get elected." – *To Jeb Bush*

"He grew up and nobody knew him. You know? When you interview people, if ever I got the nomination, if I ever decide to run, you may go back and interview people from my kindergarten. They'll remember me. Nobody ever comes forward. Nobody knows who he is until later in his life. It's very strange. The whole thing is very strange."

"Your brother's administration gave us Barack Obama because it was such a disaster those last 3 months that Abraham Lincoln couldn't get elected." – To Jeb Bush

We are led by very, very stupid people. Very, very stupid people.

"Our president will start a war with Iran because he has absolutely no ability to negotiate. He's weak and ineffective, so the only way he figures to get reelected, and as sure as you're sitting there, is to start a war with Iran."

"The man that wrote the second book ... didn't write the first book. The difference was like chicken salad and chicken shit."

"I heard he was a terrible student, terrible. How does a bad student go to Columbia and then to Harvard? I'm thinking about it, I'm certainly looking into it. Let him show his records."

"An 'extremely credible source' has called my office and told me that Barack Obama's birth certificate is a fraud"
"There is something on that birth certificate — maybe religion, maybe it says he's a Muslim, I don't know. Maybe he doesn't want that. Or, he may not have one."

"Our weak President, that kisses everybody's ass, is in more wars than I have ever seen. Now he's in Libya, he's in Afghanistan, he's in Iraq. Nobody respects us."

"I have people that have been studying [Obama's birth certificate] and they cannot believe what they're finding... I would like to have him show his birth certificate, and can I be honest with you, I hope he can. Because if he can't, if he can't, if he wasn't born in this country, which is a real possibility…then he has pulled one of the great cons in the history of politics."

"Let me tell you I'm a really smart guy. I was a really good student at the best school in the country. The reason I have a little doubt, just a little, is because he grew up and nobody knew him." *(Obama's past)*

"Our great African-American President hasn't exactly had a positive impact on the thugs who are so happily and openly destroying Baltimore."

"If Obama resigns from office now, thereby doing a great service to the country — I will give him **free lifetime golf at any one of my courses.**"

"Obamacare really kicks in in 2016. Obama's going to be out playing golf, he might even be on one of my courses. I would invite him ... I have the best courses in the world."

"I would say he's incompetent but I don't want to do that because that's not nice."

"Putin is a strong leader. He is making mincemeat out of our President."

"You look at Baltimore, you look at Cleveland. You look at all of those places, just exploding. We have an African-American president and we've never had it so bad."

"When it comes time to default, they're not going to remember any of the Republicans' names. They are going to remember in history books one name, and that's Obama."

On EVERYONE ELSE

"I'm a negotiator, like you folks." *To the Republican Jewish Coalition*

"How stupid are the people of Iowa?"

"If I were running 'The View', I'd fire Rosie O'Donnell. I mean, I'd look at her right in that fat, ugly face of hers, I'd say 'Rosie, you're fired.'"

"Robert Pattinson should not take back Kristen Stewart. She cheated on him like a dog & will do it again – just watch. He can do much better!"

"Ariana Huffington is unattractive, both inside and out. I fully understand why her former husband left her for a man – he made a good decision."

"You know, it really doesn't matter what the media write as long as you've got a young, and beautiful, piece of ass."

"Don't like @SamuelLJackson's golf swing. Not athletic. I've won many club championships. Play him for charity!"

"I have so many fabulous friends who happen to be gay, but I am a traditionalist."

"He's not a war hero. He's a war hero because he was captured. I like people who weren't captured." *(John McCain)*

"I'm very disappointed in John McCain because the vets are horribly treated in this country. I'm fighting for the vets. I've done a lot for the vets."

"Well, maybe they don't speak to the same vets that I speak to."

"Regardless of work or no work, (vets are) suffering. I'm all over the country. I see them all the time. (McCain is) virtually the head person in Washington. He's the head of the group that runs—I mean, he's—somebody's doing a bad job."

"There are some issues I don't want to say much about. I support a woman's right to choose, for example, but I am uncomfortable with the procedures. When Tim Russert asked me on Meet the Press if I would ban partial-birth abortion if I were president, my pro-choice instincts led me to say no."

"When these people walk in the room, they don't say, 'Oh, hello! How's the weather? It's so beautiful outside. Isn't it lovely? How are the Yankees doing? Oh they're doing wonderful. Great.' (Asians) say, 'We want deal!'"

"You haven't been called, go back to Univision." *(Jorge Ramos)*

"I have a great relationship with the blacks. I've always had a great relationship with the blacks."

"If Iran was a stock you should go out and buy it right now."

"Saudi Arabia, without us, is gone. They're gone."

"They better be careful or I will unleash big time on them." *(Wall Street Journal)*

"It is better to live one day as a lion than 100 years as a sheep." *(Tweet quoting Italian dictator Benito Mussolini)*

"I don't know anything about what you're even talking about with white supremacy or white supremacists. So I don't know. I don't know -- did he endorse me, or what's going on? Because I know nothing about David Duke; I know nothing about white supremacists." *(David Duke former KKK Gran Wizard)*

"I like China. I just sold an apartment for $15 million to someone from there. Am I supposed to not like them?"

"I've read hundreds of books about China over the decades. I know the Chinese. I've made a lot of money with the Chinese. I understand the Chinese mind."

On his OPPONENTS

"These people – I'd like to use really foul language. I won't do it. I was going to say they're really full of shit, but I won't say that."

Hillary Clinton –

"There's no spirit behind Hillary, there never will be. She's not going to engender spirit, there's nothing to be spirited about, and what happens is, we have something, that if we can embrace it, we're going to have a massive victory in November."

"Hillary said that guns don't keep you safe. If she really believes that she should demand that her heavily armed bodyguards quickly disarm!"

"I want to see a woman president soon, but not Hillary Clinton. She's a disaster. She's a disaster. She's a disaster. I mean, just think of the corruption and the scandal... We don't want to go through it. We want to see winning. We want to see win, win, win – constant winning. And you'll say – if I'm president... 'Please, Mr. President, we're winning too much. We can't stand it anymore. Can't we have a loss?' And I'll say no, we're going to keep winning, winning, winning... because we're going to make America great again. And you'll say, 'Okay, Mr. President. Okay.'"

"She's constantly playing the woman card. It's the only way she may get elected. I mean frankly... Personally, I'm not sure that anybody else other than me is going to beat her. And I think she's a flawed candidate. And you see what's happened recently. And it hasn't been a very pretty picture for her or for Bill. Because I'm the only one that's willing to talk about his problems. I mean, what he did and what he has gone through I think is frankly terrible, especially if she wants to play the woman card."

"They've created ISIS. Hillary Clinton created ISIS with Obama; created with Obama. But I love predicting because you know, ultimately, you need somebody with vision."

"Hillary Clinton was the worst secretary of state in the history of the United States. There's never been a secretary of state so bad as Hillary. The world blew up around us. We lost everything, including all relationships. There wasn't one good thing that came out of that administration or her being secretary of state."

"Honestly, she shouldn't be allowed to run. If that were a Republican that did what she did with the emails they would have been in jail 12 months ago. Clink!" *(Hillary Clinton)*

"Well, she has a new hairdo, did you notice that today." *(Hillary Clinton)*

"I tell you what it really was shocking to see it because you're right it must be, it was massive. Her hair became massive." *(Hillary Clinton)*

"She got shlonged, she lost, I mean she lost." *(Hillary Clinton)*

"I give to everybody. When I call, they give. And you know what, when I need something from them, two years later, three years later, I call them, they are there for me. And that's a broken system. Well, I tell you what, with Hillary Clinton, I said be at my wedding, and she came to my wedding. You know why, she had no choice—'cause I gave to a foundation that, frankly, that foundation was supposed to do good. I didn't know her money would be used on private jets going all over the world. It was."

"Do you know that Hillary Clinton was a birther? She wanted those records and fought like hell. People forgot. Did you know John McCain was a birther? Wanted those records? They couldn't get the records. Hillary failed. John McCain failed. Trump was able to get him to give something — I don't know what the hell it was — but it doesn't matter."

"I know where she went – it's disgusting, I don't want to talk about it. No, it's too disgusting. Don't say it, it's disgusting." *(Hillary's bathroom break)*

Jeb Bush –

"#JebBush has to like the Mexican Illegals because of his wife." *(deleted Tweet)*

Marco Rubio –

"Well, I think this. I think if he runs and loses and, you know, I don't think he would win right now, but if he runs and loses I think he will never be able to do anything very big politically in Florida. I don't think he would be considered by anybody as a vice president and I don't think he could ever run for governor or whatever he might want to run for in the future. So I think running and losing would be risky. But again, that's his decision. I think it has to be his decision 100 percent."

Carly Fiorina –

"Look at that face! Would anyone vote for that? Can you imagine that, the face of our next president?"

later

"I think she's got a beautiful face. And I think she's a beautiful woman."

Ben Carson -

"He said that he's pathological and he's got basically pathological disease … I don't want a person that's got pathological disease."

"It's in the book that he's got a pathological temper. That's a big problem because you don't cure that."

John R. Kasich -

"We got this one guy, he's terrible, he's the worst debater I've ever seen …He's terrible. He's terrible."

Paul Rand –

"I never attacked him on his look, and believe me, there's plenty of subject matter right there."

Bernie Sanders -

"I would never give up my microphone. I thought that was disgusting. That showed such weakness, the way he was taken away by two young women—the microphone; they just took the whole place over...That will never happen with me. I don't know if I'll do the fighting myself or if other people

will, but that was a disgrace. I felt badly for him. But it showed that he's weak."

Ted Cruz -

"She said, 'He's a pussy.'"

"And it wasn't my word, it was a word that a woman kept shouting. And she was shouting it from— and I repeated— I only repeated the word. And the place was wild. Standing ovation, everybody." *(on calling Cruz a pussy)*

"You're the basket case. Go ahead, don't get nervous."

Rick Perry –

"Rick Perry, I don't think even understands what he is saying."

The PHILOSOPHER

"The line of 'Make America great again,' the phrase, that was mine, I came up with it about a year ago, and I kept using it, and everybody's using it, they are all loving it. I don't know I guess I should copyright it, maybe I have copyrighted it."

"Rich people are rich **because they solve difficult problems.** You must learn to thrive on problems."

"If you're interested in 'balancing' work and pleasure, stop trying to balance them. **Instead make your work more pleasurable.**"

"I think apologizing's a great thing, but you have to be wrong. I will absolutely apologize, sometime in the hopefully distant future, if I'm ever wrong."

"When you're president, or if you're about to be president, you would act differently." *(on his own behavior)*

"Show me someone without an ego, and I'll show you a loser - having a healthy ego, or high opinion of yourself, is a real positive in life!"

"Just tried watching Modern Family -- written by a moron, really boring. Writer has the mind of a very dumb and backward child. Sorry, Danny!"

"If you're going to be one way and you think it's wrong, does that mean the rest of your life you have to go in the wrong direction because you don't want to change?"

On the CAMPAIGN TRAIL

"For a religious leader to question a person's faith is disgraceful. I am proud to be a Christian. … If and when the Vatican is attacked by ISIS, which as everyone knows is ISIS' ultimate trophy, I can promise you that the Pope would have only wished and prayed that Donald Trump would have been President because this would not have happened."

"I love the old days, you know? You know what I hate? There's a guy totally disruptive, throwing punches, we're not allowed punch back anymore. … I'd like to punch him in the face, I'll tell ya."

"That was so great. Who was the person who did that? Put up your hand, put up your hand. Bring that person up here. I love that." *(praise for audience members who tackled a protester)*

"Now, the poor guy — you've got to see this guy, 'Ah, I don't know what I said! I don't remember!'" *(mocking disabled NYT's reporter)*

On PROTESTERS at the RALLIES

"Part of the problem and part of the reason it takes so long is nobody wants to hurt each other anymore."

"There used to be consequences. There are none anymore."

"These people are so bad for our country. You have no idea folks, you have no idea."

"They contribute nothing. Nothing. And look at the police, they take their lives in their hands."

"I'd like to bang him."

"I'd like to punch him in the face. I tell ya."

"We have some protesters who are bad dudes."

"… the audience swung. I thought it was very, very appropriate."

"If you see someone getting ready to throw a tomato. Knock them crap out of them would you. Seriously."

"The audience hit back and that's what we need a little bit more of."

"68% would not leave under any circumstances. I think that means murder. I think that means anything."

"They're allowed to get up and interrupt us horribly and we have to be very, very gentle. They can swing and hit people, but if we hit them back, it's a terrible, terrible thing, right?"

"These are not good people, just so you understand. These are not the people who made our country great. These are the people that are destroying our country."

"Get 'em out. Get 'em out."

"He was a rough guy, and he was punching. And we had some people -- some rough guys like we have right in here -- and they started punching back. It was a beautiful thing."

On WOMEN

"I've said if Ivanka weren't my daughter, perhaps I'd be dating her."

"I think the only difference between me and the other candidates is that I'm more honest and my women are more beautiful."

"Isn't it funny that I am now #1 in the money losing @HuffingtonPost (poll), and by a big margin. Dummy @ariannahuff must be thrilled!"

"Ariana Huffington is unattractive both inside and out. I fully understand why her former husband left her for a man – he made a good decision."

"I don't have a lot of respect for Megyn Kelly—she's a lightweight. She gets out and she starts asking me all sorts of ridiculous questions and, you know, you could see there was blood coming out of her eyes, blood coming out of her wherever."

Megyn Kelly: "You've called women you don't like 'fat pigs,' 'dogs,' 'slobs,' and 'disgusting animals'..."

Trump: "Only Rosie O'Donnell."

"Rosie O'Donnell's disgusting both inside and out. You take a look at her, she's a slob. She talks like a truck driver, she doesn't have her facts, she'll say anything that comes to her mind. Her show failed when it was a talk show, the ratings went very, very, very low and very bad, and she got essentially thrown off television. I mean she's basically a disaster."

"I'd look her right in that fat, ugly face of hers and say, 'Rosie, you're fired.' We're all a little chubby, but Rosie's just worse than most of us. But it's not the chubbiness—Rosie is a very unattractive person, both inside and out."

"You know, it doesn't really matter what (the media) write as long as you've got a young and beautiful piece of ass."

"Oftentimes when I was sleeping with one of the top women in the world, I would say to myself, thinking about me as a boy from Queens, "Can you believe what I am getting?" *(2008)*

"Heidi Klum. Sadly, she's no longer a 10."

"She's been with so many guys she makes me look like a baby, OK, with the other side. And, I just don't even find her attractive. That has nothing to do with why I said it though." *(Angelina Jolie)*

"When Beyonce was thrusting her hips forward in a very suggestive manner, if someone else would have done that it would have been a national scandal. I thought it was ridiculous ... I thought it was not appropriate." *(Beyonce Knowles)*

"I don't wear a 'rug'- it's mine. And I promise not to talk about your massive plastic surgeries that didn't work" *(Cher)*

"She wanted to breast pump in front of me. I may have said that's disgusting. I thought it was terrible. She's a horrible person, knows nothing about me."

On GAY MARRIAGE

"It's like in golf. A lot of people — I don't want this to sound trivial — but a lot of people are switching to these really long putters, very unattractive. It's weird. You see these great players with these really long putters, because they can't sink three-footers anymore. And, I hate it. I am a traditionalist. I have so many fabulous friends who happen to be gay, but I am a traditionalist."

"I think the institution of marriage should be between a man and a woman. I do favor a very strong domestic-partnership law that guarantees gay people the same legal protection and rights as married people. I think it's important for gay couples who are committed to each other to not be hassled when it comes to inheritance, insurance benefits and other simple everyday rights.

"I've gone to gay weddings. I've been at gay weddings. I have been against (same-sex marriage) from the standpoint of the Bible, from the standpoint of my teachings as growing up and going to Sunday school and going to church."

On EDUCATION

"People are tired...of spending more money on education than any nation in the world per capita."

"End Common Core. Common Core is a disaster."

"Our schools aren't safe. On top of that, our kids aren't learning. Too many are dropping out of school and into the street life—and too many of those who do graduate are getting diplomas that have been devalued into "certificates of attendance" by a dumbed-down curriculum that asks little of teachers and less of students. Schools are crime-ridden and they don't teach." (2000)

"We're twenty-sixth in the world. Twenty-five countries are better than us at education. And some of them are like third world countries. But we're becoming a third world country."

On GLOBAL WARMING

"It's freezing and snowing in New York – we need global warming!"

"NBC News just called it 'The Great Freeze' — coldest weather in years. Is our country still spending money on the global warming hoax?"

"This very expensive global warming bullshit has got to stop. Our planet is freezing, record low temps, and our GW scientists are stuck in ice."

"The concept of global warming was created by and for the Chinese in order to make U.S. manufacturing non-competitive."

A very Short TWEET SELECTION

"Very sad what happened last night at the Miss Universe Pageant. I sold it 6 months ago for a record price. This would never have happened!"

"Katy Perry must have been drunk when she married Russel Brand - but he did send me a nice letter of apology!"

"If Hilary Clinton can't satisfy her husband, what makes her think she can satisfy America?" *(deleted Tweet 2015)*

Donald Trump @realDonaldTrump, at the time of this compilation has 6.79 million followers.

.

www.ingramcontent.com/pod-product-compliance
Lightning Source LLC
Chambersburg PA
CBHW032122280326
41933CB00009B/945